SOVIET
BATTLEFIELD
HELICOPTERS

SOVIET BATTLEFIELD HELICOPTERS

David Oliver

OSPREY
AEROSPACE

Acknowledgements

The author would like to thank a number of photographers for their generous assistance with the production of this book, in particular Air Marshall A A Singh (Retd), Hanspeter Abt, Patrick Allen, Robert Gretzyngier, Peter Gunti and Claudio Toselli.

Published in 1991 by Osprey Publishing Limited
59 Grosvenor Street
London W1X 9DA

British Library Cataloguing in Publication Data
Oliver, David, 1942-
    Soviet battlefield helicopters
    I. Soviet military helicopters, history
    I. Title
    623.746047

ISBN 0-85045-987-7

Editor Tony Holmes
Page design by Paul Kime
Printed in Hong Kong

Right The latest from the Mil Design Bureau, the advanced Mi-28 *Havoc* anti-tank and anti-air combat helicopter is reported to be still under development

Front cover The present and the future meet at Redhill in Surrey during Helitech '89. The Mi-35P *Hind* is perhaps the ultimate derivative of the classic Mil assault helicopter. The Mi-28 *Havoc*, seen here running up before launch, is still under development and as of 1991 hadn't been issued to service regiments (*Tony Holmes*)

Back cover Thoroughly combat tested, the Mi-24/35 family saw ten years of bitter conflict during the Soviet occupation of Afghanistan. This aircraft was photographed in more friendly skies however, the pilot enjoying the cloudless conditions over Redhill in September 1989

Title Page The menacing shape of the world's most formidable battlefield assault helicopter, the Soviet Mil Mi-24 *Hind*. This example is the Mi-35P, export version of the cannon-armed *Hind-F*. The NATO codename *Hind* is unknown to the Soviets who christened the Mi-24 the Hunchback or Sturmovik

For a catalogue of all books published by Osprey Aerospace please write to:

The Marketing Manager, Consumer Catalogue Department Osprey Publishing Ltd, 59 Grosvenor Street, London, W1X 9DA

Introduction

When introducing Soviet Battlefield Helicopters it is perhaps appropriate to recall that the founder of the United States' helicopter industry, Igor Ivanovich Sikorsky, was born in Kiev, in the Soviet Union, 102 years ago.

However, the vast territories of the Soviet Union might have been specially created for the helicopter and development of the modern battlefield helicopter began in 1947 when Stalin asked Mikhail Leontievitch Mil, Chief of the TSAGI Helicopter Laboratory (the Soviet equivalent of RAE Farnborough) to submit proposals for a small military utility helicopter.

Two proposals, those of Yakovlev and Mil, were accepted for evaluation, both of which were built and ready for testing by September 1948. The Mil Design Bureau's first helicopter, the Mi-1 was selected for quantity production in 1950, followed two years later by the larger Mi-4, some of which still remain in operational service today. Long before the West, the Mil Bureau saw the possibilities of arming helicopters and after early attempts to install anti-tank missiles on the Mi-1, the Mi-4 carried both rocket launchers and gun pods.

In June 1960 the classic Mi-8 made its first flight. Featuring pressed spar rotor blades with an electrothermal de-icing system for all weather operations, main rotor hydraulic dampers, four-channel autopilot and twin-engine safety, the *Hip* compared well with its Western contemporaries.

It soon became the Soviet workhorse from which were developed the Soviet Navy's amphibious anti-submarine Mi-14, the Mi-17 and the fearsome *Hind* multirole combat helicopter. Along with the MiG-21 fighter, the ferocious looking Mi-24 *Hind* came to represent the 'Red Menace' to many, and like the United States' Huey in an earlier conflict, became the symbol of the Soviet Union's involvement in the Afghanistan war.

The *Hind*'s successor, the Mi-28 *Havoc*, represents the zenith of Soviet battlefield helicopter design and if glasnost succeeds it may well be the last of the line of Mil helicopters that hold no less than 96 International World records and, ironically, have twice been awarded the Sikorsky Trophy by the American Helicopter Society.

Right Built in larger numbers than any other military helicopter, including the ubiquitous Huey, the Mil Mi-8/17 family are operated by more than 30 countries. Illustrated is a Yugoslavian Air Force *Hip-C* armed with UV-16-57 rocket launchers

Contents

The 'Hunchback'

The latest version of the Mi-24, the *Hind-E,* is distinguished by the sensor probes at the side of the gunner's front cockpit. This helicopter belongs to the 49th Combat-Attack Helicopter Regiment of the Polish Air Force, based at Pruszsz-Gdanski

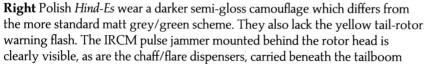

Right Polish *Hind-Es* wear a darker semi-gloss camouflage which differs from the more standard matt grey/green scheme. They also lack the yellow tail-rotor warning flash. The IRCM pulse jammer mounted behind the rotor head is clearly visible, as are the chaff/flare dispensers, carried beneath the tailboom

Above The rear view of this Czechoslovakian *Hind-D* shows the four UV-32-57 rocket launchers carried under the stub-wing and the AT-2 *Swatter* anti-tank missile rails under the tips

The *Hind-D* has seen service with more than a dozen air forces aside from the WarPac countries. Two tandem blown canopies cover separate cockpits for the pilot and gunner. A four-barrel 12.7 mm gun is mounted in a chin-turret beneath the gunner's front cockpit, the weapon being flanked on either side by small blisters which contain a forward-looking infra-red sensor (FLIR)/TV and radar dish. An electro-optical low-light (LLTV) sensor is mounted on the port wing-tip

Left As it hovers inches above the ground at Kbely air base near Prague, the large area of exhaust from this Czechoslovakian Mi-24, known locally as the Crocodile, can be clearly seen against the trees in the background

Above With every available hatch and door agape a Czechoslovakian Mi-24 *Hind-E* undergoes maintenance at Pilsen air base

A line-up of Czechoslovakian Mi-24 *Hind-Es* of the 11th Helicopter Regiment, based at Pilsen in Bohemia. The four hard points under the stub wing and the AT-3 Spiral anti-tank missile rails under the wingtips are clearly visible in this rear view

Right Eight fully-equipped troops, plus reloads for its own weapons launchers, can be carried in the Mi-24's spacious main cabin. On the *Hind-D* the pilot's entry door opens to the right and the gunner's to the left. Besides being heavily armoured, the pilot's door also has a map stowage bag fitted on the inside

Below The Hungarian Air Force has operated the Mi-24 since the early 1980s, some 40 *Hind-D/Es* being based at Veszprem

Twenty-four Mi-25s equip No 125 Squadron of the Indian Air Force. The export version of the *Hind-D,* the helicopters are finished in a dark green/brown semi gloss camouflage. Several *Hinds* recently saw service in Sri Lanka where they operated as part of the Indian Peace Keeping Force

Right A Hungarian *Hind-D* makes a low-level high speed run over the airfield with its tricycle landing gear retracted. The 60 ft 8 in (18.5 m) long Mi-24 has a top speed of over 200 mph (320 km/hr)

Above Known to the Mujahideen guerillas as the 'Devil's Chariot', hundreds of Soviet Mi-24s of all variants were deployed to Afghanistan between 1979 and 1989. Illustrated is a *Hind-F*, finished in a weathered tropical camouflage scheme, and photographed during the Soviet withdrawal from Kabul in February 1989. Dozens of *Hinds* were passed to the Afghanistani Air Force after the withdrawal, these helicopters now being used regularly against the rebels

Left More than 2000 *Hinds* had been produced by the end of 1990 and production continues at two facilities at Arenyev and Rostov. Seen here in tropical camouflage is the latest export version of the *Hind-F*, the Mi-34P

Below 'Red 11' made history as the first Soviet combat helicopter to land in the UK

Right The aggressive front-end of the latest Mi-24 variant. The *Hind-F* is armed with twin-30 mm cannon mounted on the right side of the helicopter one above the other. Initial airframe and acoustic vibration caused by firing the guns was eliminated by extending the muzzle adaptors beyond the nose of the helicopter

Above The *Hind-F's* large anhedral stub-wings give only a limited amount of lift, but are able to carry up to 3307 lbs (1500 kgs) of weapons, including four 80 mm rocket launchers and four AT-6 *Spiral* radio-controlled anti-tank missile launch tubes

Above Powered by two 2200 shp Isotov TV3-117 turboshafts, the *Hind* was developed from Mil's multirole Mi-8 *Hip*

Right Topping the *Hind*'s bulky mid section is a fully articulated main rotor hub of machined steel. Beneath the stub-wing is the heavy duty main landing gear which retracts straight back and up into the fuselage

An in-flight view of *Hind-F's* 80 mm rocket launchers carried under the port stub-wing. A venerable weapon dating from the 1960s, the launchers are seen through the main cabin armour plated windows that open inwards, and are held agape by powerful clamps to provide ventilation, or a clear line of fire from within the cabin

Some idea of the size of the *Hind* can be gauged from these in-flight shots of the Mi-34P. The diameter of the five-bladed main rotor is 55 ft 9 in (17 m), giving it a rotor area of nearly 2500 sq ft. Its overall length with rotors turning is 68 ft 11 in (21 m)

Left Mil's awesome *Hind-F* hovers menacingly overhead. The long-stroke twin-wheel nose gear which gives ground clearance for the numerous chin-mounted sensors is clearly visible

Above The squat bulk of the *Hind-F*, a helicopter which made its first public appearance in the West during Helitech '89, held at Surrey's Redhill Aerodrome

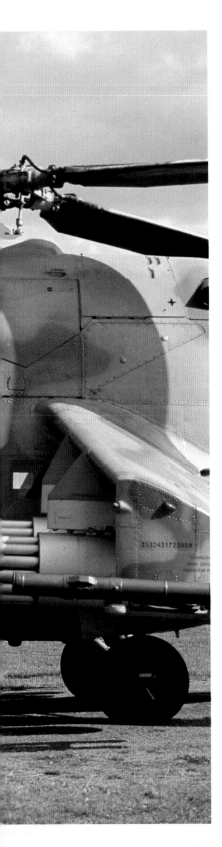

Left The crew of 'Red 11' go through their pre-engine start checks at Redhill. The small exhaust port above the red star insignia belongs to the powerful auxiliary power unit (APU) mounted transversely aft of the main gearbox

Below A picture of power and strength. Known in the Soviet Union as the Hunchback, the Mi-24/5 has a normal take-off weight of 24,692 lbs (11,200 kg), a large percentage of this figure being due to the extensive conventional and composite armour around the engine compartments and cockpit sides. The canopies have flat armour-glass windscreens and the engines have inlet shields to prevent ingestion of ice or sand

Above Waiting on a green field in Surrey, the crew of the Mi-35 prepare to show the *Hind* off to the British public at Helitech '89

Right *Hind-F's* twin 30 mm cannon were designed for tank-busting but proved particularly effective at suppressing ground fire in Afghanistan. The FLIR/TV sensor below the gun barrels is protected by powerful spring-loaded armoured doors when not in use

Havoc

Mil Design Bureau's tandem two-seat anti-armour anti-air combat helicopter, the Mi-28 *Havoc*, first flew in 1982 and had a protracted development before attaining quantity production in 1991

41

Left and above In the air, the Mi-28 bears a superficial resemblance to the American AH-64 Apache. Although both helicopters share similar dimensions, the Mi-28 can be identified by its five-bladed main rotor, shorter stub wings and asymmetric horizontal stabilizer, with the tail rotor positioned on the right

Above Havoc seen against the English sunset during its UK debut at Helitech

Above right Shown in the 'flesh' at the 1989 Paris Air Salon before photographs had even been released in the West, the Mi-28 appeared in both the static and flying displays at Le Bourget

Below right Seen taxying out at Le Bourget prior to commencing its flying display, the *Havoc* surprised many observers with its incredible manoeuvrability. The auxiliary power unit (APU) outlet between the two downward deflected exhaust covers is clearly visible in this rearward view

The stepped cockpits are heavily protected with flat armour-plated panels, the gunner occupying the front seat and the pilot the rear. Access to the pilot's position is through a car-type door on the starboard side with the gunner's door hinging to port

Left The 'grinning' face of the Mi-28 belies its power and punch. Below the nose-mounted radar is the open FLIR/TV window and the chin-mounted 30 mm cannon. The shoulder-mounted engines have hemispherical inlet shields to deflect FOD and reduce radar signature

Below Each of the Mi-28's 8 ft (2.35 m) anhedral stub wings give little positive lift but can carry an 80 mm rocket launcher and up to eight AT-6 *Spiral* anti-tank missiles. Above the stub wing is the engine IR suppressor

Above The *Havoc*'s formidable chin-mounted 30 mm cannon can traverse, plus or minus, 110 degrees from side to side, 13 degrees up and 40 degrees down, and is controlled by the gunner's helmet-mounted sight

Right The backward-kneeling main wheels are fitted with heavy duty tyres for rough field operations. In the event of a crash landing the main landing gear is designed to absorb vertical descent shock-loads of up to 49.2 ft (15 m) per second. A novel method of Mi-28 crew protection is the provision of parachutes and inflatable egress chutes on the cockpit side to enable both crew members to slide clear of the airframe and landing gear before deployment of the parachutes

Above Consisting of two separate blades, the tail rotor on the *Havoc* has suffered from severe design problems, the helicopter's service entry being delayed as a result

Above left To save weight, composite technology has been extensively used in the Mi-28's construction, the five-bladed main rotor, engine covers, tail rotors and horizontal stabilizer all being made of lightweight material. Unique in modern helicopter design is the titanium cockpit side protection and ceramic underside armour. Powered by two 2200 shp Isotov TV3 turboshaft engines, the *Havoc* boasts a take-off weight of 22,950 lbs (10,400 kg) and a maximum speed of over 190 mph (310 km/hr)

Below left Although not designed as a troop carrier, the Mi-28 has a small passenger cabin in its deep fuselage with enough room for two ground crew. The port access door can be seen below the downward-deflected exhaust covers

Multifarious Mils

Right Arguably the world's most successful military helicopter, more than 10,000 examples of the Mil Design Bureau's powerful and rugged Mi-8 *Hip* were built before production switched to the upgraded Mi-17. A true workhorse, the Mi-8 is equally at home in deserts or, as in this case, the extreme cold of the Arctic Circle. This is one of several *Hips* operated by the Finnish Air Force

Below Powered by two 1700 shp TV2-117A turboshafts, the Mi-8 multirole transport can accommodate up to 28 fully armed troops or 12 stretchers. This example, operated in the search and rescue role by the Finnish Air Force, has been specially fitted with a chin-mounted search radar, hydraulic rescue hoist over the main aft-sliding door and searchlights on the main landing gear strut. These 'bolt on' extras were provided by the Finnish aircraft manufacturer Valmet to an Air Force specification

Right The Mi-8 is fitted for icing conditions with electrically-heated windscreens and rotor blades and bleed-heated engine inlets. This Finnish Air Force *Hip* is housed in an immaculate heated hangar at Rovaniemi, inside the Arctic Circle

Above The colourful unit badge on the SAR *Hip* identifies it as belonging to the Finnish Air Force's Lapland Wing, based at Rovaniemi

Left The extensively glazed nose provides excellent visibility from the Mi-8's flight deck, a feature of the design which is greatly appreciated by Finnish Air Force crews when operating in white-out conditions

Right and below The basic Mi-8T passenger version, identified by its large square windows, is operated by paramilitary organizations such as the Czechoslovakian Border Police, as illustrated here. The diameter of the five-bladed rotor is 69 ft 10 in (21.29 m), and the fuselage length 59 ft 7 in (18.17 m)

Above The Yugoslavian Air Force operates some 30 Mi-8s mainly in the troop transport role. This weathered *Hip-C* is configured for 'grunt shunting' duties, hence the large circular windows in the fuselage

Right This Yugoslavian *Hip-C* is carrying UV-16-57 rocket launchers on its standard twin stores rack

Left A non-standard high-gloss olive green and sky-blue scheme is worn by this Yugoslavian Air Force *Hip-C*

Below The tail rotor warning on the rear boom of this Yugoslavian Air Force Mi-8 is in Serbo-Croat

Left and above Hungarian Mi-8TBs are used mainly for army support. This *Hip-C*, finished in standard WarPac camouflage, is being refuelled at Budaors airfield near Budapest. The large pod running along the side of the fuselage is an external fuel tank

Another *Hip-C* belonging to the fragmenting WarPac. This East German Air Force Mi-8TB belongs to *Transporthubschraubergeshwader* 24, based at Brandenburg-Briest near Potsdam

Left A pair of East German Mi-8Ts in formation over Holdzdorf air base, located 50 miles south of Berlin. The second *Hip*, 'Black 931', wears SAR colours, and is fitted with a doppler radar in the box under the tailboom. However, unlike 'Black 626', the SAR *Hip* is devoid of the external twin-stores racks

Below The future of this immaculate East German Hip-C is very much in doubt following German reunification at the end of 1990

Above Described as the world's most heavily armed helicopter, the Mi-8TBK *Hip-E* carries an awesome encyclopedia of weaponry. This East German People's Navy (*Volksmarine*) variant has a nose-mounted 12.7 mm DShK machine gun, six UV-32-57 launchers carrying a total of no less than 128 rockets and four AT-2 *Swatter* anti-tank, or in this case anti-ship missiles

Left The formidable weapons capability of the *Hip-E* is clearly illustrated here, this particular Mi-8 carrying AT-2 *Swatter* missiles above the outboard rocket launcher. Mounted above the cabin door is a 331 lb electric rescue hoist, whilst inside the *Hip* itself is a long-range fuel tank, firmly strapped to the floor

Left This distinctive dark blue *Hip* of the East German *Volksmarine* helicopter wing 'Kurt Barthel', based at Parow in north east Germany, is used for coastal surveillance over the Baltic

Below Following reunification, East German *Volksmarine Hips* are being used in the more passive search and rescue role along the Baltic beaches. 'Black 907' has been fitted with a more powerful rescue hoist

Above One of three Mi-8 *Hip-Cs* operated by *Grupo* 3 of the Peruvian Air Force at Callao. Once a large operator of the Mi-8, the Peruvian Army withdrew them from service due to their unsuitability for hot and high conditions

Left Conversely, the Pakistani Army has successfully operated the *Hip* in hot and high conditions for a number of years. The two-tone sand and stone camouflage scheme on this helicopter is similar to that worn by the Peruvian Mi-8

This Indian Air Force Mi-8 *Hip-C*, seen flying over New Delhi in VIP colours, is used to transport government ministers in and around the capital

Left Seen against the dramatic backdrop of the Himalayas, this Indian *Hip* is finished in a more standard olive drab scheme. One of ten Mi-17s ordered by the IAF for operations from mountain bases, this helicopter has a doppler radar in the orange housing under the tailboom and provision for an IR jammer aft of the rotor head

Above A pair of Soviet Mi-17 *Hip-Hs* in tropical sand and stone camouflage and Aeroflot markings seen operating from Gondar airstrip, a remote base located some 8000 ft above sea level in Ethiopia's central highlands

Right A group of six Ethiopian Air Force Mi-8s wearing sand and earth camouflage are seen with an anonymous sand and stone Mi-17 at Addis Ababa air base

Above A British Army Air Corps Gazelle AH.1 of No 7 Flight, based at Gatow in West Berlin, shadows a Soviet Mi-17 electronic warfare (ECM) *Hip-K* along the East/West German border only a few months before the notorious Berlin Wall was breached

Previous pages, left and above Carrying six UV-32-57 rocket launchers, an IR jammer and a chaff/flare dispenser strapped to the rear tailboom, this Mi-17 *Hip-H* has only been in service with the Polish Air Force since 1988. Assigned to the Krakow helicopter regiment, this Mi-17 wears a distinctive unit badge on its fuselage

Starting up at it base at Pilsen, this Mi-17 *Hip-H* is carrying only a single UV-32-57 rocket launcher on its triple weapons rack. Its parent group is the 11th Helicopter Regiment which is equipped with a mixed force of 35 *Hinds* and 12 *Hips*

Left The latest version of the *Hip*, the Mil-17-VA, appeared at a number of international airshows in 1989 including the Helitech at Redhill

Above The Mil-17-VA at the 1989 Paris Air Salon was parked alongside the massive bulk of the world's largest aircraft, the An-225 *Cossack*

Fitted out as a flying ambulance by Technika of Hungary, this Mil-17-VA is powered by two 1900 shp Isotov TV3-117VM turboshafts. Access to the 7 ft 8 in (2.34 m) long by 5 ft 10 in (1.8 m) wide main cabin is via the full-section rear clamshell doors fitted as standard to all *Hip* variants. Fully kitted out with a self-contained, Honda powered, operating theatre, as well as an electrocardiographic unit and an incubator, the Mil can carry up to four patients

The Mil-17, which made its Western debut at the 1985 Paris Air Salon, can be distinguished from its predecessor by the shorter engine nacelles and port-side tail rotor. The *Hip-C* has a maximum speed of 155 mph (250 km/hr) and a range of 289 miles (465 km)

Hook and *Halo*

Although Mil's Mi-6 heavy transport helicopter made its first flight more than 30 years ago, more than 300 still serve with half a dozen air forces, this particular aircraft serving in the Soviet Union

Right The Mi-6 *Hook* was the largest, fastest and heaviest production helicopter in the world when it first appeared. The diameter of its five-bladed main rotor is 114 ft 10 in (35 m), length of the fuselage 108 ft 10 in (33.18 m), maximum speed 186 mph (300 km/hr) and it can carry a maximum internal payload of 26,455 lb (12,000 kg), Soviet *Hooks* are armed with a single nose-mounted 12.7 mm DShK machine gun

Above Six Mi-6s are operated by *Escuadron* 341 of the Peruvian Air Force's *Grupo* 3 at Lima-Callao. The *Hook* was the first Mil design to feature twin turbine engines mounted above the fuselage, thus giving the helicopter an unobstructed load area within its 39 ft (12 m) main cabin. This unarmed Peruvian Mi-6 has the 50 ft 2 in (15.3 m) span detachable stub wings removed and a chin-mounted radar fitted

Almost 20 years after the appearance of the *Hook*, the Mil Design Bureau produced the heaviest and most powerful helicopter ever flown. With the load carrying capacity of a C-130 Hercules, the Mi-26 *Halo*, powered by two 1400 shp Lotarev D-136 turboshafts, has a maximum payload of 44,090 lbs (20,000 kgs) and can carry 82 fully equipped troops. India was the first export customer for the massive Mi-26, the Air Force eventually receiving ten of the behemoth Mils. Seen here unloading supplies at a remote Himalayan Indian Army outpost, this *Halo* has its full section rear clamshell doors and vehicle ramp open. The louvred inlet doors for the APU, mounted beneath the flight deck floor, are also clearly visible

Right All ten Mi-26 heavy transport helicopters are operated by No 126 Squadron of the Indian Air Force's Western Command, based at Awantipur. The type was extensively used by the Indian Peace Keeping Force in Sri Lanka

Below The Mi-26T's pressurized flight deck accommodates the pilot, co-pilot, navigator and flight engineer. The cockpit side windows are blistered to enable the crew to see the main wheels from the flight deck

Halo, designed by M N Tishchyenko (who took over the Mil Design Bureau after M I Mil's death in 1970), made its Western debut when one of the five development aircraft was shown at the 1985 Paris Air Salon

Above With a main rotor diameter of 105 ft (32 m), tail rotor diameter of 25 ft (7.75 m) and an overall fuselage length of 110 ft (33.73 m), the Mi-26 is by far the largest helicopter ever to attain quantity production. Despite its maximum take-off weight of 123,457 lbs (56,000 kg), the *Halo* has a maximum speed of 183 mph (295 km/hr)

Right Distinguishing features of the Mi-26 include the massive eight-bladed main rotor, the engine inlet particle deflectors and the large circular cooling fan inlet between the engines. The twin main-wheel gear can be raised or lowered hydraulically when on the ground to adjust the rear door height for ease of loading. Two 5511 lb (2500 kg) electric winches on full length ceiling rails are fitted in the unpressurized main cargo hold

Utilities

First flown in 1961, the Mil-2 *Hoplite* multirole light helicopter has been produced solely in Poland by PZL-Swidnik. The largest customer for the PZL Mi-2 has been the Soviet Union, the helicopter being used for liaison, scouting and training. These colourful *Hoplites* belong to the Soviet Defence Society (DOSAAF), a sort of auxiliary air force

More than 5000 Mi-2s have been delivered by Swidnik. Powered by two licence-built 444 shp Isotov GTD-350P turboshafts, the *Hoplite* can carry six passengers or four stretchers and an attendant. A 287 litre auxiliary fuel tank was attached to the left side of the cabin on all the DOSAAF helicopters that visited the UK in 1986

The Mi-2 has a maximum speed of 124 mph (220 km/hr) but a limited range of only 106 miles (170 km) on internal fuel, hence the need for the bolt on tanks

A Soviet team of six Mi-2 *Hoplites* from the DOSAAF helicopter training organization attended the 1986 World Helicopter Championships held in the grounds of the English stately home of Castle Ashby, Bedfordshire

Above *Hoplite*'s wide spread main wheels and twin-wheel nose gear provide a stable platform when landing or manoeuvring on rough ground. The familiar Mil cooling-fan duct for the engine and gearbox oil system radiator is clearly visible above and between the two engines

Right Ten Mi-2 *Hoplites* serve with the Czechoslovakian Border Police along with a similar number of Mi-8 *Hips*. They are based at Prague's Ruzyne Airport

The latest version of the PZL-Swidnik *Hoplite*, the Mi-2B (with improved navaids), serves with the Polish Air Force. Modified to serve as a communications jamming platform, this camouflaged *Hoplite* has an additional aerial array fitted above and below the national insignia

Several Polish derivatives of the Mi-2 have been produced in prototype form, including this version powered by two 650 shp Allison 250-C30B turboshafts

Fitted to the basic Mi-2 airframe, the US Allison engines gave a considerable boost to the *Hoplite*'s performance, but the difficulties in acquiring the engines in the late 1980s led to the project being shelved. Now that Poland has thrown off its WarPac loyalties it may be revived

The ultimate development of the 30 year old Mi-2 is the PZL-Swidnik W-3 *Sokol (Falcon)*. First flown in 1979, the *Sokol* has a larger redesigned fuselage that can accommodate 12 passengers, as well as a new four-bladed main and three-bladed tail rotor made of glassfibre construction. Two 858 shp Glushenkov 10W turboshafts give it a maximum speed of 146 mph (235 km/hr) and a range of 422 miles (680 km). Illustrated is a *Sokol* operated by the Polish Naval Aviation in the search and rescue role

In 1951, Stalin instructed M I Mil to produce a 12,000 lb (5443 kg) helicopter and have it flying in a year. Nine months after conception, in May 1952, the Mi-4 *Hare* assault transport made its first flight. Although similar in design to the US Sikorsky S-55 Whirlwind, it was much more powerful, and is still serving today with a number of air forces including China, where it was built under licence, Mongolia and the Soviet Union

Left Recently retired from the Czechoslovakian Air Force, this camouflaged *Hare* is fitted with a ventral gondola for the navigator/observer

Overleaf The Mi-4 *Hare* was powered by a 1700 hp Shvetsov ASh-82V 14-cylinder radial piston engine which gave it a top speed of 130 mph (210 km/hr) and a range of 250 miles (400 km). Twelve fully-armed troops could be carried in its main cabin, the *Hare* also having rear clamshell doors for loading bulky cargoes like small vehicles. This example was flown to the United States by a defecting Cuban pilot